COOKING CHEMISTRY
WHY DO FRUITS AND VEGGIES TURN BROWN?

by India James

pogo

Ideas for Parents and Teachers

Pogo Books let children practice reading informational text while introducing them to nonfiction features such as headings, labels, sidebars, maps, and diagrams, as well as a table of contents, glossary, and index.

Carefully leveled text with a strong photo match offers early fluent readers the support they need to succeed.

Before Reading

- "Walk" through the book and point out the various nonfiction features. Ask the student what purpose each feature serves.
- Look at the glossary together. Read and discuss the words.

During Reading

- Have the child read the book independently.
- Invite them to list questions that arise from reading.

After Reading

- Discuss the child's questions. Talk about how they might find answers to those questions.
- Prompt the child to think more. Ask: Have you ever seen brown fruits or vegetables? What kinds were they?

Pogo Books are published by Jump!
3500 American Blvd W, Suite 150
Bloomington, MN 55431
www.jumplibrary.com

Copyright © 2026 Jump! International copyright reserved in all countries. No part of this book may be reproduced in any form without written permission from the publisher.

Jump! is a division of FlutterBee Education Group.

Library of Congress Cataloging-in-Publication Data is available at www.loc.gov or upon request from the publisher.

ISBN: 979-8-89213-843-7 (hardcover)
ISBN: 979-8-89213-844-4 (paperback)
ISBN: 979-8-89213-845-1 (ebook)

Editor: Katie Chanez
Designer: Anna Peterson

Photo Credits: Leinemeister/Shutterstock, cover; ferigrinjoe/Shutterstock, 1; Natalia Marshall/Shutterstock, 3; EdnaM/iStock, 4; kzww/Shutterstock, 5 (apples); Maglara/iStock, 5 (background); BartTa/Shutterstock, 6; Artem Kutsenko/Shutterstock, 7 (foreground); Kueakoon T/Shutterstock, 7 (background); nito/Shutterstock, 8–9 (foreground); HAKINMHAN/Shutterstock, 8–9 (background); Sinhyu Photographer/Shutterstock, 10–11; Anna Om/Shutterstock, 12–13; Maria_Usp/Shutterstock, 14–15; pong-photo9/iStock, 16–17 (hand); baibaz/Shutterstock, 16–17 (fruit); onurdongel/iStock, 16–17 (background); Shutterstock, 18–21; Igor Kovalchuk/Shutterstock, 23.

Printed in the United States of America at Corporate Graphics in North Mankato, Minnesota.

TABLE OF CONTENTS

CHAPTER 1
Yum to Yuck! 4

CHAPTER 2
Browning Basics 6

CHAPTER 3
Let's Experiment! 18

ACTIVITIES & TOOLS
Try This! 22
Glossary 23
Index 24
To Learn More 24

CHAPTER 1
YUM TO YUCK!

It is snack time. You slice a juicy apple. Yum!

But after a while, the slices turn brown. Yuck! What happened?

CHAPTER 2
BROWNING BASICS

Fruits and vegetables are also called produce. Brown produce does not look good. Its **texture** may be different than when it was fresh. Some brown foods feel mushy. How does this happen?

Fruits and veggies have a skin or peel. This outer layer protects the inside. The peel or skin keeps air and **bacteria** out. It also helps keep water in.

skin

CHAPTER 2

Browning often starts after fruits and vegetables are cut open. Why? **Oxygen** in the air mixes with the food's **enzymes**. A **chemical** called melanin is made. Melanin has a brown color. It changes the color of the food.

DID YOU KNOW?

Slicing produce causes the water inside to slowly **evaporate**. The produce starts to dry out. This makes fruit less juicy. Vegetables are less crisp. They may not taste as good.

CHAPTER 2

CHAPTER 2

Old produce browns, too. How? All living things are made of **cells**. Cells have walls. In plants, these usually stop oxygen from reaching the enzymes. But the cell walls get weak as they age. The produce becomes soft. Weak cell walls let air into the food. Brown spots appear.

cell wall

TAKE A LOOK!

How do fruits and vegetables turn brown? Take a look!

1. Produce ages or is sliced open. Air gets in.

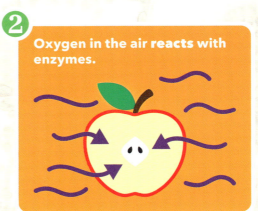

2. Oxygen in the air **reacts** with enzymes.

3. Melanin forms. It gives the food a brown color.

CHAPTER 2   11

Different types of produce brown at different times. Why? The amount of oxygen and enzymes matter. So does the temperature of the room. Warm produce browns faster than cold produce. Refrigerating food can slow browning.

DID YOU KNOW?

A sliced apple may brown in just a few minutes. A cut-up potato takes about 30 minutes. A banana peel browns two to five days after leaving the store.

CHAPTER 2

Citrus fruits, such as oranges, take longer to brown. Why? These fruits have a lot of **citric acid**. This keeps oxygen and enzymes from mixing quickly.

CHAPTER 2 15

Brown produce is not usually bad for you. But there are ways to keep your food looking fresh! Lemon juice can help. Why? It has citric acid. Covering food also helps. This keeps air away.

DID YOU KNOW?

Browning can be good! It gives some foods and drinks color and **flavor**. These include some tea leaves. It is also done with coffee beans and cacao beans!

CHAPTER 2   17

CHAPTER 3
LET'S EXPERIMENT!

Let's experiment and stop fruit from turning brown!

What You Need:
- ¼ cup (60 milliliters) vinegar
- ¼ cup (60 mL) lemon juice
- 2 tablespoons (30 mL) honey
- 1 cup (237 mL) water
- ¼ cup (60 mL) pineapple juice
- apple
- paper plate
- pencil
- four bowls
- knife or apple slicer
- cutting board
- spoon

START WITH THESE STEPS:

1

Pour the lemon juice, vinegar, and pineapple juice into their own bowls. Mix the honey and water in the fourth bowl.

2

Divide the plate into five sections. Label one section for each bowl. Label the last one "plain."

CHAPTER 3

3

Ask an adult to cut the apple into five slices. Set one slice in the "plain" section.

4

Dip one apple slice in each bowl. Put it by its label.

CHAPTER 3

5

Leave the apple slices out for one hour.

6

When you come back, what do you see? Is one slice more brown than the others? Taste the slices. Does one taste better than the others?

CHAPTER 3

ACTIVITIES & TOOLS

TRY THIS!

KEEP IT FRESH

There are other ways to keep fruit from turning brown. Find out how with this fun activity!

What You Need:
- two apples
- knife or apple slicer
- cutting board
- plate
- rubber band

1. Ask an adult to cut each apple into slices.
2. Lay one set of apple slices on a plate.
3. Put the slices of the other apple back together. Use a rubber band to keep them in place.
4. Come back in an hour. Compare the two apples. How are they different?

GLOSSARY

bacteria: Microscopic, single-celled living things that exist everywhere.

cells: The smallest units of living things.

chemical: A substance that has specific characteristics and can interact with other chemicals to change form.

citric acid: An acid found in foods, such as citrus fruits, that is used to flavor foods and keep them fresh.

citrus fruits: Acidic, juicy fruits such as oranges, lemons, limes, and grapefruits.

enzymes: Proteins produced by plants or animals that cause chemical reactions.

evaporate: To change into a gas.

flavor: Taste.

oxygen: A colorless gas found in air and water that humans and animals need to breathe.

reacts: Changes chemically by mixing substances together.

texture: The way something feels.

ACTIVITIES & TOOLS   23

INDEX

age 10, 11
air 7, 8, 10, 11, 17
bacteria 7
cell walls 10
citric acid 14, 17
citrus fruits 14
covering 17
cut 8, 13, 20
dry out 8
enzymes 8, 10, 11, 13, 14
flavor 17
fresh 6, 17

melanin 8, 11
mushy 6
oxygen 8, 10, 11, 13, 14
peel 7, 13
refrigerating 13
skin 7
slice 4, 8, 11, 13
soft 10
taste 8, 21
temperature 13
texture 6
water 7, 8, 18, 19

TO LEARN MORE

Finding more information is as easy as 1, 2, 3.

❶ Go to www.factsurfer.com
❷ Enter "fruitsandveggies" into the search box.
❸ Choose your book to see a list of websites.

24 ACTIVITIES & TOOLS